The
Meditation
Coloring
Book

The Meditation Coloring Book

ARCTURUS

ARCTURUS

This edition published in 2016 by Arcturus Publishing Limited
26/27 Bickels Yard, 151–153 Bermondsey Street,
London SE1 3HA

ISBN: 978-1-78428-283-7
CH005102NT

Printed in China

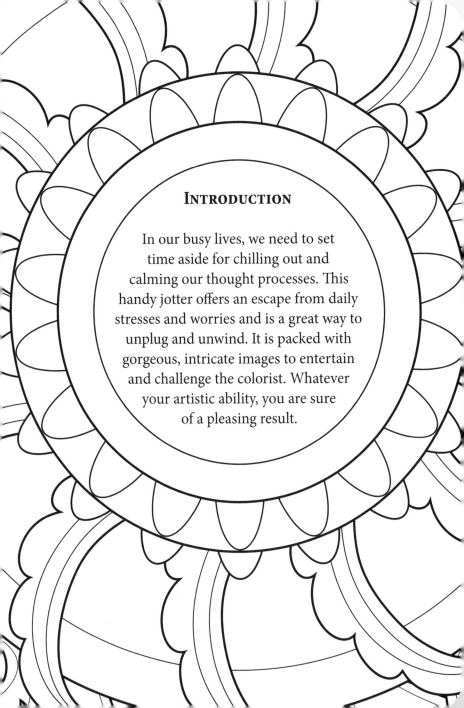

INTRODUCTION

In our busy lives, we need to set time aside for chilling out and calming our thought processes. This handy jotter offers an escape from daily stresses and worries and is a great way to unplug and unwind. It is packed with gorgeous, intricate images to entertain and challenge the colorist. Whatever your artistic ability, you are sure of a pleasing result.

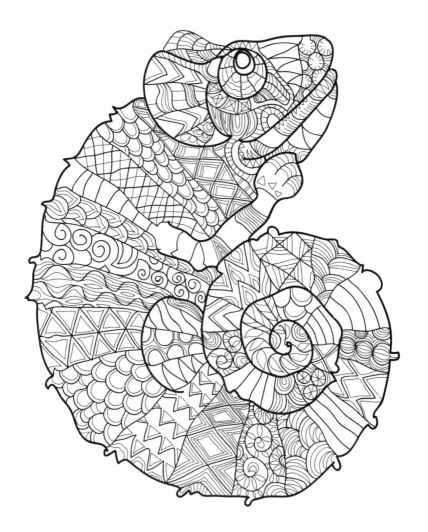

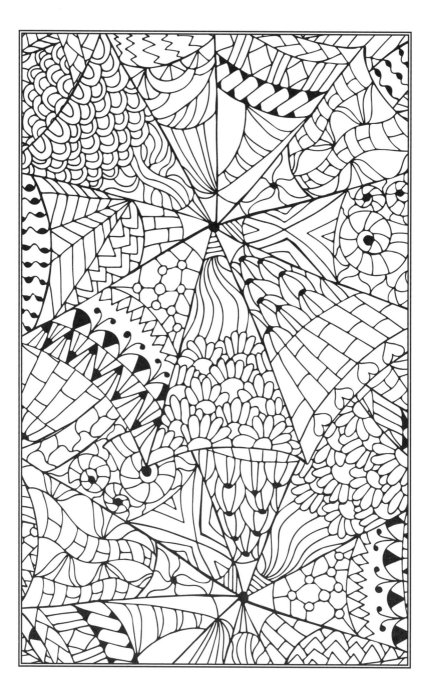

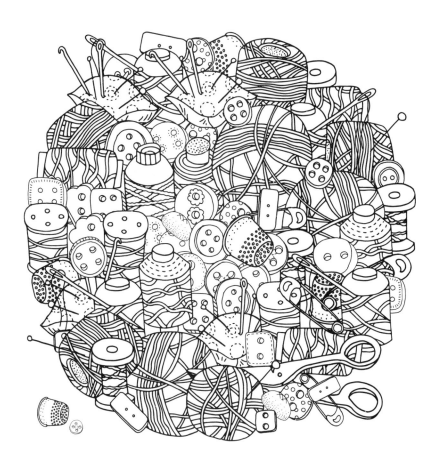

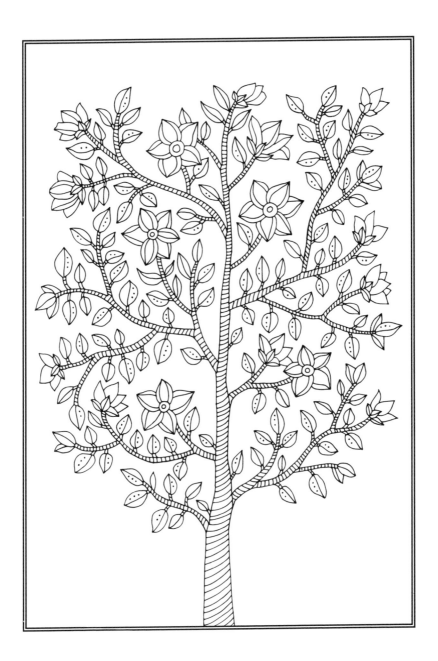